FARM ANIMALS

SHEEP

Ann Larkin Hansen

ABDO Publishing Company

visit us at
www.abdopub.com

VK EW HB

Published by Abdo Publishing Company 4940 Viking Drive, Edina, Minnesota 55435.
Copyright © 1998 by Abdo Consulting Group, Inc. International copyrights reserved in all countries. No part of this book may be reproduced in any form without written permission from the publisher.

Printed in the United States.

Cover Photo credits: Peter Arnold, Inc.
Interior Photo credits: Peter Arnold, Inc.

Edited by Lori Kinstad Pupeza

Library of Congress Cataloging-in-Publication Data

Hansen, Ann Larkin.
    Sheep / Ann Larkin Hansen.
    p. cm. -- (Farm animals)
    Includes index.
    Summary: An overview of sheep, their history, habits, care, and usefulness by giving us wool.
    ISBN 1-56239-606-4
    1. Sheep--Juvenile literature. [1. Sheep.] I. Title. II. Series: Hansen, Ann Larkin. Farm animals.
    SF375.2.H35 1998
    636.3--dc20
                                        96-709
                                        CIP
                                        AC

About the Author

Ann Larkin Hansen has a degree in history from the University of St. Thomas in St. Paul, Minnesota. She currently lives with her husband and three boys on a farm in northern Wisconsin, where they raise beef cattle, chickens, and assorted other animals.

Contents

Sheep Were First

Do you see those white sheep on the green hill? They are busy turning grass into meat and **wool**. The **lambs** play tag around their mothers. The **shepherd** walks through to check that all is well. Sheep were the first **domesticated** animal to provide food for people. For ten thousand years or more, shepherds and their dogs have watched over sheep.

Opposite pages:
A herd of sheep.

Sheep and People

Sheep have been **domesticated** so long that no one is sure who their wild ancestors were. There were sheep herds and **shepherds** before there were farms and villages.

Early tribes of men in the Middle East guided their sheep as they moved between winter and summer **pastures**. The men protected the sheep from wolves and other predators. In return, sheep gave the tribe meat and **wool**.

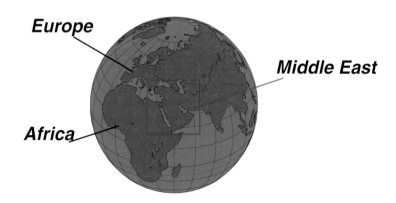

Europe

Middle East

Africa

Sheep have been providing wool for people for a long time.

Types of Sheep

Today there are more than 200 **breeds** of sheep. Some, like the Merino, are used for their **wool**. Others, like the Suffolks, are raised mostly for meat. A few are milked like a cow! The milk is used to make fancy cheeses.

The **fleece** of a sheep may be long or short, thick or fine, depending on the breed. Usually, it is white, but every once in a while black sheep are born.

Opposite page:
Churro sheep in
New Mexico.

What Sheep Are Like

Sheep are timid and small enough to be easily handled. **Ewes**, the mother sheep, weigh between 125 and 250 pounds (57 to 113 kilograms). The **rams**, the father sheep, may weigh as much as 350 pounds (159 kilograms), and will **butt** you if you aren't careful.

Each sheep grows an average of eight pounds (3.6 kilograms) of **wool** each year. Sheep have knobby knees and long heads, and some **breeds** have horns. The tail is usually cut short, to keep flies from laying eggs under it.

Opposite page: A lamb resting in a pasture.

Sheep and Grass

Sheep are made for **grazing**. Like cattle, they have no upper front teeth, just hard pads. With their lower teeth they press grass and clover against their upper pads and rip it off. With their sensitive lips and small mouths, they can graze plants right down to the dirt.

Sheep have four stomachs.

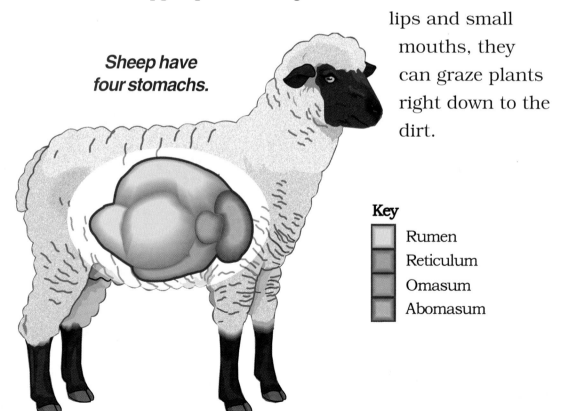

Key

- Rumen
- Reticulum
- Omasum
- Abomasum

Sheep are **ruminants**, or **cud**-chewers. The grass is stored in the first stomach until they lay down, burp it up, and chew it again. After the cud is well chewed, it is swallowed to be digested in the second, third, and fourth stomachs.

Sheep can graze on grass all day long.

Sheep Are Tough

A sheep's thick **fleece** protects it from cold winters, but is too warm in very hot weather. Split hooves make it easy for a sheep to climb rough and rocky land. Sheep can use land that is too rough or too dry for raising crops and cattle.

Sheep cannot defend themselves very well. Coyotes, wolves, wild dogs, and other predators love to eat sheep. **Shepherds** use dogs, fences, and sheds to keep their **flocks** safe.

Opposite page: Sheep can climb rough and rocky land and their thick wool keeps them warm in cold weather.

15

Caring for Sheep

Sheep need very little shelter. If it is very wet or very hot, a nice shed helps. Sheep need **pasture** or hay, but very little grain. As with all farm animals, fresh water, salt, and minerals must be available. Like horses and dairy cattle, sheep need to have their hooves trimmed regularly. This is just like cutting your fingernails. It doesn't hurt, and makes walking much easier.

Opposite page: Sheep only need a pasture for grazing and a fence to keep out predators.

Keeping Sheep Healthy

Shepherds work hard to keep their **flocks** healthy. Sheep need regular **vaccinations** for several diseases. They must be dipped or sprayed to kill **parasites** in their skin and **wool**. They must also be given medicine several times a year to kill worms that live inside their bodies.

Most importantly, sheep must keep moving to fresh **pasture**. Otherwise they will kill the grass.

Opposite page: Shepherds work hard to keep their flocks healthy.

19

Lambing Time

Most **ewes lamb**, or give birth, in the spring. This is the busiest time of year for the **shepherd**. When a ewe is ready to lamb, the shepherd puts her in a small pen. Sheep are more likely to have difficult births than other farm animals, and the shepherd must be alert.

Each new lamb is wiped down, and checked to make sure it is breathing and warm. The shepherd must watch to see that the ewe lets it nurse.

Opposite page: A ewe with her newborn lamb.

Getting Started

Sometimes **lambs** are too cold or weak to nurse. Sometimes the mother has too many. The **shepherd** stays busy warming up lambs, helping them nurse, and finding new mothers for the **orphans**.

Ewes must be tricked into accepting a baby that is not their own. A good shepherd knows many tricks, but sometimes a new mother just can't be found. Then the lamb must be fed with a bottle.

Opposite page: A farmer bottle feeding a lamb.

Growing Up

After all the **lambs** and **ewes** have had a chance to get to know each other, they are turned out to **pasture**. The mothers "baaa" to their babies to keep them close. But the lambs just want to play.

Through the summer the lambs gain as much as one and a half pounds (.7 kilograms) each day. They make a lot of noise when they are brought in to be wormed and **vaccinated**. By the next spring, they are adults.

Opposite page: Lambs playing together on a hilly pasture.

Shearing

Before lambing in the spring, the **ewes** have their heavy winter coats **sheared** off. When the **shearer** arrives, the sheep are put in a pen, and brought to him one by one. With an electric clippers, the **wool** is off in minutes.

Helpers clip the matted parts off the **fleece**, then roll and tie it. The rolls of fleece are packed into special wool sacks. The 250-pound (113-kilogram) sacks are sent off to be carded, spun, and turned into sweaters, socks, coats, carpets, and other beautiful things.

Opposite page: Sheep shearing doesn't hurt the sheep.

27

Glossary

Breed—different kinds of the same animal; like different flavors of ice cream.

Butt—to hit with the head.

Cud—wads of grass burped up from the first stomach of a ruminant for chewing into a finer mass before final digestion in the other three stomachs.

Domesticated—tamed by man.

Ewe—adult female sheep.

Fleece—a sheep's coat of wool.

Flock—a group of sheep that live together.

Graze—to eat grass, clover, and other plants.

Lamb—baby sheep. Also means a ewe giving birth.

Lanolin—the natural oil of the fleece. It is used for lotions, salves, ointments, and many other things.

Orphan—a lamb that has lost its mother.

Parasite—a life form that lives in or on other animals and injures their health.

Pasture—an open, grassy area.

Ram—adult male sheep.

Ruminant—a grazing animal with four stomachs that chews cud.

Shear—to cut the fleece off the sheep.

Shearer—a person specially trained to shear sheep.

Shepherd—a sheep herder, or one who cares for the sheep.

Vaccination—a shot given with a needle to prevent disease.

Wool—the hair of the sheep. Also refers to the yarn and cloth made from the fleece.

Internet Sites

The Virtual Farm
http://www.manawatu.gen.nz/~tiros/ftour1.htm
A very impressive display including photos and sound. This site is all about dairy farming in New Zealand.

Museums in the Classroom
http://www.museum.state.il.us/mic_home/newton/ project/
Prairie Chickens and the prairie in Illinois by Mrs. Vanderhoof's third grade class and Mrs. Volk's fourth grade science classes.

Goats
http://www.ics.uci.edu/~pazzani/4H/Goats.html
This site has photos, graphics, and sound. It has tons of information on raising goats and it even has a goat game.

Virtual Pig Dissection
http://mail.fkchs.sad27.k12.me.us/fkchs/vpig/
Learn how to dissect a pig without hurting a pig. This is a really cool site that gets a lot of traffic.

Sheep
http://www.ics.uci.edu/~pazzani/4H/Sheep.html
This site has everything you would want to know about sheep. Why raising sheep is fun, the sounds sheep make, sheep statistics, basic care, sheep supplies, and much more.

Castalia Llamas
http://www.rockisland.com/~castalia/cllama.html
Chosen as a hotsite, featured on TV, listed in Popular Science's WebWatch. Full of llama facts, images and stories to amuse and bewilder. This is a cool site, check it out.

These sites are subject to change. Go to your favorite search engine and type in "farm animals" for more sites.

PASS IT ON
Tell Others What You Like About Animals!
To educate readers around the country, pass on interesting tips about animals, maybe a fun story about your animal or pet, and little-known facts about animals. We want to hear from you!
To get posted on ABDO Publishings website, E-mail us at "animals@abdopub.com"

Index